IN MEMORY OF MY LATE NIECE,
TERESA MONAHAN,
WHO WELCOMED ALL WITH LOVING ARMS.

...

"Life is the childhood of our immortality."
Johann Wolfgang von Goethe

Publisher's Note: While MariVi's experiences reflect the real life feelings and general experiences of many immigrant children and families in the United States, this is a work of fiction. Names, characters, places, and incidents are either the product of the author's imagination or used fictitiously, and any resemblance to actual persons, living or dead, businesses, events, or locales is entirely coincidental.

Text and illustrations © 2025 by MariVi & Company LLC
Published in 2025 by MariVi & Company LLC. All rights reserved.

No portion of this book may be reproduced, in print or by electronic means, stored in a retrieval system, or transmitted in any form or by any means without prior written permission from the publisher. If you are interested in using or sharing text or illustrations from this book, or using MariVi or other characters in this book, please contact the publisher by email at marivi@wearemarivi.com.

MariVi the Master Navigator

All Aboard

by
Maria (Lopez) Twena

Illustrated by Amy E. Ubelhor

• • •

MariVi and those like her feel alone in the world, living somewhat
as outsiders even from their most intimate communities,
constantly balancing two languages and two cultures.
As we go through our challenging childhoods and young adulthoods,
she is here to guide us with empathy, wisdom, and humor,
giving us perspective and strength for our journeys.

MariVi reminds all of us, especially children of immigrants,
that we are not alone.

CONTENTS

• • •

1.	NEWS & SPELLING BEE	**7**
2.	LUNCH WITH FRIENDS	**13**
3.	THE BUS & HOME	**17**
4.	GAME NIGHT	**26**
5.	THE ARRIVAL OF MIRIAM	**30**

My name is MariVi. I am 8 years old and am in third grade.

My parents came from another country, and they speak a different language, Spanish. I am the only one in my family who was born here. I am different from them—my own family. I am also different from my friends at school. Not only because I don't **look** like my friends, but because my family doesn't **act** like their families either.

My parents don't speak English very well, so I always translate for them, as if I were the parent, but I'm not. And when they speak Spanish to me outside our home and others hear them, I get nervous.

I can't wait to grow up, be on my own, and belong somewhere.

But for now, I'll enjoy third grade, time at home with mi familia, and continue to navigate two different worlds.

• • •

When I returned to school, I was nervous, but not as nervous as when I had started first grade. Summer had been nice, but I was starting to get bored. I still had to help clean the house and go to the supermarket with Mama on the weekends, but I also got to play a lot with Isa and Gordo, and watch TV, but I missed some of my new friends. I only saw Karen once when we ran into each other at the supermarket, and I saw Debbie only once at mass, from far away. We both waved at each other.

I had a new teacher, a new classroom, and new things to learn. And I didn't know then I'd also be making a new friend.

• • •

1
NEWS & SPELLING BEE

One day at school, right before the Christmas holidays and the new year, my teacher, Mrs. Herbert, announced that we would have a new student starting school later in the year, and that she would be visiting us with her family soon. Mrs. Herbert looked a lot older than my first-grade teacher, Mrs. Smith and my second-grade teacher, Mrs. Haskell. She wore black glasses that hung from a chain around her neck, shoes with small heels, and a skirt (with pantyhose), every single day. Her voice was different too. Deeper and stronger than Mrs. Smith's. And she always wore a skirt and matching jacket, and she never wore pants. Her hair

didn't move either. It looked like she put a lot of hair spray on her hair in the morning, just like Mama did to me. I was a little scared of her *all the time*. She would get mad quickly and would raise her voice loudly, like Mama does at the supermarket when I don't hear her.

When she told us we'd have a new student joining us, everyone in class started asking her questions. Is it a boy or a girl? "Girl." Where is she from? "Her family just moved here from New York." Wow, I thought, New York!? I had always heard that New York was big and had big buildings and lots of people walking everywhere, all the time. And I knew, because Isa had told me that there was a special statue that floats in the water—a Lady. I don't know how she stands in the water without drowning, but she does. I forget what she's called, but she's supposed to be tall and has a crown on her head. She said she also is holding a book and is there to welcome new people that arrive to this country. I'd like to go there someday, I thought, and see the Lady. I guess you must sail into the country to be truly welcomed here.

When we asked Mrs. Herbert the name of the new student, she replied: "Miriam," and left it at that. No last name, just

Miriam. I had never heard that name before but thought it was pretty, and that it sounded like Mary.

I couldn't wait to meet Miriam. I remembered that in first grade even though all of us were new to the school, I felt like I was the only *new* person because I looked different than the rest of the students and because my parents spoke a different language, Spanish. I wondered how it would be for Miriam.

Mrs. Herbert then said it was time to work on our words and Spelling. I was so happy. I loved Spelling. It was my favorite subject in school. It was the only time that I could stand up in class and speak and not feel any butterflies in my tummy. NONE! I liked to sound out the words, imagine what the letters would be in my head, and write them down to see if I was right. It was a lot of fun!

My favorite words were words that were made up of two words. I think my teacher called them compound words. It's one full word, next to another full word and it makes up a brand-new word. My favorite words that I had learned so far this year were: sunshine, baseball, pancake, raincoat, and birdhouse.

Mrs. Herbert asked us to try to put five of our favorite compound words into a story, and then share it with the class. I came up with: "My family woke up to sunshine and pancakes, then went to a baseball game after passing a birdhouse. It started to rain so we put on our raincoats." The class clapped at my story when I had finished. They really liked it. I tried not to be nervous when I read it and spoke loudly so Mrs. Herbert wouldn't ask me again to raise my voice, like she had the last time I shared my sentence. And Mrs. Herbert said: "Well done, MariVi!" and gave me a gold star. She hadn't said that to anyone else that day, so I was feeling happy and wanted to go home to show Abuelita and Mama.

I didn't know whether to tell Mrs. Herbert that we don't eat pancakes in the morning. We also don't have a birdhouse and have never been to a real baseball game, but I guess it didn't matter. It was all made up anyway. I wasn't sure if that was okay or if it was something bad. I am going to ask Abuelita when I get home, I thought. She'd know if it was okay.

After class was over, I asked Mrs. Herbert why Spelling Bees are called Spelling Bees. She said that they started more than two hundred years ago and that the Bees had to do with a word that goes back to people helping people do things. I don't know what that has to do with bees that buzz and sting, so I just nodded and said: "Okay, thank you."

I now wanted to get home to see if Papa and Mama did Spelling Bees in Spanish when they were growing up.

After Spelling, we did some Reading and Writing, then it was lunchtime, then we had Math and ended our day with Social Studies, which was becoming my second favorite subject.

I liked to learn about different people around the world. It made me feel less different.

• • •

2
LUNCH WITH FRIENDS

I was very happy to see that for lunch today Mama had made me a sandwich. It was a ham sandwich and all it had on it was ham and mayonnaise. It was made with my favorite bread which was white and very soft. The same bread that I would toast when I would get home from school for a snack. But for lunch, it wasn't toasted, and I liked it a lot that way.

I liked to flatten it with my hands and then eat it. Sometimes the mayonnaise gushed out of the sandwich and made a mess, but I would clean it up. I liked mayonnaise a lot.

Mama still hadn't made me any chocolate chip cookies but had given me a banana for dessert. She had offered to put in a piece of chocolate flan, but I said "*No, no quiero,*" (No, I don't want any) when she asked. Even though that was one of my most favorite desserts. I didn't want to have anything in my lunch that was different than anyone else's ever again. And flans are gooey so you can't eat them with your fingers, like sandwiches. You need a fork. I didn't want to have a fork at lunch. No one at school who brought lunch from home used a fork.

I think Abuelita had heard us talking about lunch, because after I ate my sandwich and banana, and picked up my brown bag to throw it away, I felt there was still something under one of my many napkins that Mama always put in my bag, that I hadn't used. When I lifted my napkin, under it was a small piece of chocolate candy. My favorite! I didn't see her do it, but she did. I loved Abuelita.

Lunch was a lot of fun. I always sat next to Karen and Debbie. I guess you could say that they were my best friends now. We had been in the same class the last two years, and were now in third grade together. We always had fun. And today, like most days, we wanted to eat quickly and get out to recess to get some popcorn and play freeze tag and jump rope. Because we liked jump rope so much, we needed to get out to recess early to be first in the popcorn line then first to grab the jump ropes – there weren't that many at school. Instead of all going together, I told them we should split up today. I could get the jump rope and they could get the popcorn. They said it was okay. I also wanted some time with the jump rope by myself but didn't tell them. I wanted to practice a little.

I was getting good at jump rope. I used to skip just once every time the rope came back around which made me very tired very quickly. That's how Papa jumped rope and he was the one who had taught me. But last year, Karen

taught me to skip once, then do a baby skip. That was a LOT easier. And since there were three of us, two of us could hold both ends of the rope and walk away from each other to create a lot of space, then one of us would jump in the middle. We'd take turns to see how many jumps we could do. Debbie was the BEST at that, but I was watching her carefully to see how I could do better.

I think because she was a little shorter than Karen and me, she could get the rope around her head faster. But I wasn't sure.

• • •

3
THE BUS & HOME

After school, I met up with Isa and Gordo in the cafeteria to wait for our bus. We had decided last year to always sit at the exact same table in the cafeteria while we waited for the bus. Isa was talking to her friends and Gordo had decided not to sit with us but to play 'cabbage ball' (which is like baseball, but the ball is big like a cabbage – that's what Debbie told me) outside on the playground with his friends. I didn't see Karen or Debbie so I was going to ask Isa if I could go outside and watch Gordo play. And just as I was going to, I heard the lady call "38 Third", then **"All Aboard!"** over the microphone. The lady was using a VERY LOUD microphone so you could hear her from far away.

Gordo came running to get in line and was all sweaty and stinky. On the bus, I sat next to Isa like I always did, but this time she insisted on sitting next to the window, so I had to sit on the aisle, away from the window. Gordo sat behind me, and he was hitting the back of my seat with his feet. I told him to stop, or I was going to tell Mama when we got home. I also whispered: "You really smell." He looked at me and said: "And you smell in the morning when Mama puts hairspray on your hair!" I couldn't believe he had said what he said and that he said it so loudly. The boys sitting around Gordo started laughing out loud which hurt my feelings. I felt like I was going to start crying and a lump formed in my throat.

I told Isa: "Make him stop, Isa." Isa turned around and said: "Gordo, if you don't stop you are going to be in a lot of trouble when we get home." Gordo looked at Isa and said: "I don't care." But he must have cared a little bit because he stopped hitting the back of my seat.

While we were getting close to home, I told Isa that I wanted to tell Mama, Papa and Abuelita that I was only going to speak English at home from now on. I didn't want to speak Spanish and that I loved learning *and* speaking English. It made me feel like I belonged here.

Isa looked at me with a smirk on her face then started laughing out loud. Isa said: "Good luck with that, MariVi. I told them I didn't want to speak Spanish at home after my first week of first grade and they didn't like it. Mama told me that even though I'm American on paper I'm not American at all. I'm Latina. And that I should be proud of my culture. It made me feel bad for even asking. I think you shouldn't ask her because it's only going to make her mad."

I told Isa: "I was born here, Isa, you weren't." And Isa responded, "I really don't think that matters. I came here when I was very young. It's the same thing." I thought to myself but didn't say out loud: "No, it isn't."

As soon as we got home the Spanish began. Abuelita had my warm chocolate milk ready for me in the kitchen and had two toasts getting ready to pop out of the toaster. *"¿Como pasaron el día, mis cariños?"* (How did you all spend your day, my loves?) As soon as I said: *"Bien, Abuelita"* and kissed her, I realized that if I only spoke English in the house, Abuelita wouldn't understand me, and I wouldn't be able to speak with her. That wouldn't be good. I LOVED Abuelita.

I decided to not say anything. Maybe Isa was right. Mama would get upset and Abuelita and I wouldn't be able to

talk to each other. Neither would Mama and I. Okay, bad idea, I thought.

Mama came into the kitchen to kiss us hello and give us a hug. "*¿Como estuvo tu almuerzo MariVi? ¿Te gusto tu sándwich de jamón?*" (How was your lunch, MariVi? Did you like your ham sandwich?) "*Si, Mama,*" I replied. "*Me gustó mucho.*" (I liked it a lot.) Then I turned to Abuelita and whispered: "*Gracias, Abuelita, por el chocolatico. Estaba muy rico.*" (Thanks, Grandmother, for the piece of chocolate. It was delicious.)

Mama then quickly turned to Gordo and asked him how his day was and gave him a big hug. Her face then changed from being happy to being serious. She told Gordo: "*Tienes que ir a bañarte, Gordo. Estas apestoso.*" (You need to go bathe, Gordo. You are smelly.) Gordo grumbled something under his breath and replied: "*Si, Mama. Despues de mi bocadillo.*" (Yes, Mama. After I have my snack.)

Gordo then opened the refrigerator, served himself a big slice of chocolate flan and poured himself a glass of white milk, with some help from Mama. He ate the flan in no time, then went to bathe as he licked the milk stains all over his mouth and made a face at me.

Boys are gross, I thought.

As he passed me, I said: "See, I told you you were smelly." And Gordo looked at me and said: "Thank you, LacaVi (Hair Spray Vi)!!!" He and Isa both started laughing loudly. I quickly turned to Mama who briefly smiled then stopped when she saw that I was looking at her. I didn't like it and started biting my lip, then decided it was better just to go to my room before I started crying.

He made up the name LacaVi because he had made fun of how much **laca** (hair spray) Mama puts on my hair in the morning. So instead of calling me MariVi, he called me LacaVi!!!!

Mama told Gordo, *"Ya es suficiente, Gordo. Vete a bañar."* (That's enough, Gordo. Go bathe.) Mama NEVER punished Gordo. He could do anything and not get in trouble. She adored him.

I didn't think anyone had noticed me go into my room with my feelings hurt.

Then I heard a small tap on the door. It opened and Abuelita peaked inside. *"¿Estás bien, cariño?"* (Are you okay, my dear?) *"Si, Abuelita. Gracias."* (Yes, grandmother. Thank you.). She then placed my uneaten toast and warm chocolate milk on my desk, then started to shut the door so that I could change into my play clothes.

As she walked out, she said: *"No te preocupes con las tonterías que dice Gordo. Así son los niños."* (Don't worry about the rubbish that Gordo says. That's how kids are.)

I stopped Abuelita before she got to the door: *"¿Abuelita, si hay que escribir una oración en la clase, y no es de verdad, es un pecado?"* (Grandma, if you must write a sentence in class and it's not true, is it a sin?) Abuelita didn't understand why I was asking or what had happened in class, so I explained it to her and told her my sentence, or at least what I had remembered. *"No, mi amor. No es un pecado. Despreocúpate y felicidades por tu oración. Eres muy creativa, y también muy sensitiva."* (No, my love. It's not a sin. Don't worry about it and congrats on your great sentence. You are very creative and very sensitive.)

She then hugged me and left the room.

I played with Renata a little bit, finished my toast and milk, then went to the living room to watch some TV after putting my plate and glass in the kitchen. Gordo was taking a bath and Isa had gone to our room to change so the TV was all mine.

I watched some cartoons and was laughing for a while, then I must have fallen asleep.

...

4
GAME NIGHT

The next thing I remembered was Papa coming home from work and the excitement that came with that.

At dinner, which was a little different tonight because Abuelita had decided that she wanted to cook and Mama had let her because she was busy organizing closets and preparing bags of clothes to give away to a new family that had arrived from another country, I asked Papa and Mama about Spelling Bees and if they had them at school when they were young.

Papa said: "*No, nunca he oído de los Spelling Bees. En nuestro país no hacíamos Spelling Bees. A lo mejor es porque nuestro idioma es más fácil de entender y se escribe como suena. El inglés es más difícil. Y muchas veces no se escribe como suena.*" (No, I've never heard of Spelling Bees. In our country, we didn't have them. Maybe it's because our language is easier to understand and is written just like it sounds. English is harder. Many times, it isn't written like it sounds.) Mama agreed. "*Tampoco me acuerdo de este ejercicio en la escuela.*" (I too don't remember this exercise in school.)

Papa spoke English more than Mama. He had a heavy accent when he spoke, but he understood it a lot better. I asked him why he spoke it better than Mama and Abuelita, and he said it was because he worked outside of the house and Mama and Abuelita just worked in the house, so they didn't need to use English a lot.

When dinner was finished and we had all completed our homework, Abuelita wanted to play dominoes. I liked to play, but Gordo and Isa thought it was boring, so they said they weren't interested. Papa said he'd play for a little bit and Mama agreed too, so we all sat down to play.

I don't remember EVER playing a game with Papa, Mama and Abuelita, just us four. It was a lot of fun. They were all very different when playing a game. Abuelita was very serious and quiet, as was Papa. Mama was always excited if she won a game, which she did this time. I almost told her she sounded like she had won the lottery, something else she liked to play. But I didn't. And they all "passed" differently. In dominoes you need to "pass" if you don't have a domino that you can throw down in the game. To pass, you need to gently hit the table with your domino. Papa always knocked on the table once, like when he jumped rope, Abuelita knocked once and a half, the second knock much lighter, almost sounding like an echo of the first knock – just like the sound the wooden spoon made when she was cooking and had just finished stirring the pot and was hitting it to drop any food still stuck on the spoon. And Mama knocked on the table twice, loudly, always – just like when she would tell us to pick up after ourselves – "MariVi! MariVi!"...

I never said anything to them, but I thought it was funny that they each did it their own way.

・・・

5
THE ARRIVAL OF MIRIAM

On a Friday morning, right before school started, a new girl walked into our classroom with her parents. My desk was very close to Mrs. Herbert's so I could see them when they walked in. I had gotten to school early that day and was studying words for the Spelling test Mrs. Herbert gave us every Friday.

The girl was different than anyone I had seen in school before. Her skin was a pretty color. It was a lot like mine, but had more of a yellow color, and she had long, very thick hair, all the way down her back, and freckles on her face. I think her hair was even thicker than mine! It was brushed into a beautiful braid, and I wondered if her mom used hairspray when she brushed her hair that morning. She also wore pink glasses which were small and round.

Her parents were very tall. Her father had light brown hair and wore black glasses. Her mother was very dark and tall too. She had big eyes, beautiful white teeth and wore a dark skirt with a light sweater. Her hair was cut straight all the way around her head, from ear to ear, and was much curlier than mine. And she wore pretty earrings and lots of bracelets on her left arm.

Mrs. Herbert presented Miriam to the class, along with her parents Adela and Rob. She said Miriam would be joining us next year in school but was in town this week, so her family had decided to visit our school. Miriam's last name was Cohen. I tried to figure out how to spell it, and then Mrs. Herbert wrote it on the chalk board. C-O-H-E-N, a lot like it sounded. But I would have guessed C-O-H-I-N.

Mrs. Herbert said: "Class, this is going to be our new student I told you about, Miriam Cohen, and these are her parents. I'd like you all to make her feel welcome. Miriam is going to spend a little time in class with us today, while her parents meet the principal." All the students clapped loudly. I looked at Karen and Debbie and Joseph and Steve, as they were watching Miriam and felt like I did my first day of school. I secretly hoped Miriam wasn't feeling like she didn't belong in school like I had in first grade. She kept looking at the floor and not at us. And her parents were right next to her! She must be shy I thought. Just like me.

And then Mrs. Herbert looked at me and said: "MariVi, I think you will see that you and Miriam have a lot in common." I didn't know what she was saying. Was she saying that I looked like Miriam because we were darker than the other kids? I just know that I felt pain in my tummy and felt like I was going to cry because now all my friends and classmates were staring at ME, not Miriam. I felt like I was in first grade again.

Then just when I was going to lower my head to act like I was studying, Miriam's mom, Adela, took a couple of steps closer to my desk, lowered herself so that her face was looking right at mine and said, *"Buenos Dias, MariVi."* (Good Morning, MariVi.)

I didn't know what to do. I felt so bad that I just wanted to disappear. I didn't want anyone to know that I spoke Spanish and hadn't told anyone that we were Spanish. The kids found out in first grade when I had my accident because Mama came in speaking in Spanish, but I had hoped that no one remembered. I NEVER spoke Spanish at school and didn't want to speak Spanish again. I didn't want to be different.

But I had to say something to Miriam's mom. It wouldn't be nice not to. And if Mama found out that I didn't say anything, I would get in trouble.

So, I raised my head and looked at her and whispered: *"Buenos días, Señora."* (Good morning, Ma'am.)

As I said it, I realized that her Spanish sounded a little different than mine. I don't know why, but it did. It sounded almost like a song.

Then I quickly looked at Miriam who had kept her head down but had raised her eyes to see if I would say something to her mom. She nodded at me a little as if to say that she understood and gave me a small smile. She had a pretty smile and was missing two teeth, just like me!

Miriam's parents then quickly left the classroom, after kissing her good-bye, and Mrs. Herbert sat Miriam right next to me. I gave her a small wave and she waved back. Then I started biting my lip. I always did that when I felt strange. And my left leg started shaking. I don't know why I was feeling like this. Miriam's parents had already left the classroom. I think I just started feeling like I wasn't supposed to be there, and now I had to be nice to Miriam because her mom spoke Spanish.

I wondered if Miriam spoke Spanish too. And if she spoke Spanish to both her mom and dad. I didn't hear her father speak Spanish at all. He had told me 'Good Morning', not *'Buenos Días'*. I wondered if he knew how to speak it. I wanted to ask her, but class had started, and I wouldn't be able to speak with her until lunch time.

I looked at Miriam from the side of my eye. She was pretty in a different way. I noticed that she wore a necklace too, but it didn't have a cross on it. It looked like it had a hand on it. I wasn't sure if that's what it was or if my eyes were playing tricks on me, but that's exactly what it looked like.

Mrs. Herbert then came up to me and quietly asked me to be Miriam's buddy. I first thought to myself, 'That's not fair, I didn't have a buddy when I started school.' But then I remembered that in first grade nobody did, because we were all new to the school.

I said, "Yes, ma'am, Mrs. Herbert." I wasn't sure what a buddy was supposed to do so I quietly asked Mrs. Herbert. She told me a buddy is someone that new students can talk to and one that can help them around the classroom, explain the schedule to them, etc. She thought I would be great because Miriam could speak Spanish AND English, just like me.

That's when I REALLY started biting my lip. I didn't want to help Miriam in Spanish. That's NOT what I wanted to do. But my teacher said I had to, so now I needed to be Miriam's buddy whether I wanted to or not.

The bell for school to begin had already rung but we were all still getting ready for class to start. I could reach out to Miriam easily as she was sitting on my left, so I leaned over and said in English, "Miriam, if you need anything, let me know. I can help you." She looked at me and said, "Thank you, MariVi," with a very soft voice – barely a whisper.

I wanted Miriam to know that I preferred to speak English, that's why I spoke to her in English.

There was something about how she said 'thank you' that made me feel bad for wishing I didn't have to help her. She was very sweet. And shy, just like me. She looked at me as if she felt bad that she needed help, and I remembered what first grade was like when I had started school. And how bad I felt for needing help and being different. Then I don't know what happened to me, but I felt that I HAD to help Miriam make it in school okay. And that I wanted to help her. I didn't want anyone to ever feel like they didn't belong. It was a bad feeling. So, I thought to myself, whatever Miriam needs, I will be here for her.

Mrs. Herbert then announced that we were going to start the day with our Spelling quiz. 'Yay' I thought to myself. This is my favorite subject and I spent time looking at the words and practicing how to spell them, so I was ready for the quiz. Mrs. Herbert said Miriam didn't have to take the quiz, but if she wanted to write down the words while Mrs. Herbert called them out, she could.

Mrs. Herbert started calling out words: 'won't, isn't, football, rainbow, house, book, and they.' These were

SO easy, I thought to myself. I finished very quickly and looked over at Miriam to see how she was doing. She was finished too! I guess she liked Spelling like I did. *We're going to be great friends, I thought to myself.*

Mrs. Herbert then picked up everyone's quiz and asked the class to take out their books so we could begin Reading. She gave Miriam a book and I leaned over to show Miriam where we were in our story. It felt good to help Miriam.

Before I knew it, it was time to go to lunch. I asked Miriam if she wanted to sit with me at lunch and she said: "Yes, MariVi." I noticed that when she said MariVi, she was twirling the 'r' in MariVi. Not many people can do that if they don't speak Spanish.

I hadn't asked Karen and Debbie if it was okay for Miriam to sit with us. I guess I just thought it would be.

As everyone went to the cloak room to grab their lunches, I saw that Miriam had a brown bag for lunch too, just like me. But it wasn't in the cloak room. Her mom had given it to her, and I hadn't seen it.

When she pulled out her brown bag, I noticed that someone had put a happy face on it – I never got a happy face on mine. I thought whoever did that must really love her. I wondered if she would have Spanish food in her lunch or if she would have English food but didn't want to ask.

As we lined up to go to lunch, I waved to Miriam to come stand next to me, and Karen and Debbie. I wasn't sure if this was the right thing to do. I felt that Karen and Debbie weren't happy about our new classmate, but if they weren't, they didn't say anything.

As we sat at the table for lunch, there were only three chairs on the table. Karen and Debbie sat down without thinking of Miriam. I grabbed the chair from the table next to us and put it next to mine, so that we would both be facing Karen and Debbie. Karen and Debbie weren't sure what to do.

I watched carefully as Miriam opened her lunch. She had a sandwich in hers, just like mine. Mine was a ham sandwich and hers was a turkey sandwich, I think. I didn't want to ask. She too had a banana in hers, and much to my surprise, she had a chocolate chip cookie for dessert.

I wondered about Miriam. Where is she really from? My teacher said New York, but her Mama had to be from somewhere else. Does she know Spanish? Was it the first language she learned at home? Does her father speak Spanish? What has school been like for her in New York? Will she be like me and want to learn? Does she have any brother or sisters?

I thought to myself that Miriam and I might become friends. But as I looked at Karen and Debbie, and their faces, I wasn't sure. They didn't seem so happy to have Miriam sitting at our lunch table.

'El tiempo lo dirá' (Time will tell), as Abuelita would say.

• • •

ACKNOWLEDGEMENTS

MariVi was conceived 15+ years ago in the SF Bay Area. Many individuals have loved her, encouraged her every step, and breathed life into her spirit when it was waning. It does indeed take a village; mine has been selfless and bountiful.

• • •

To my late mother-in-law, Eunice, whose self-reliance and Protestant work ethic taught me a lot about what it is to be a traditional American, giving me the opportunity to more deeply discern the differences between the collectivist spirt and the self-reliant ethos.

To my daughter, Frankie. You have often said that MariVi is 'my song'. Thanks for listening to it on repeat and supporting her along her path – and singing her theme song as well.

To my husband, Yacov, who understands the reality of a bicultural existence as well as I do, thanks for your wisdom and for putting up with the long hours and commitment that developing a series takes.

And to MariVi's illustrator, Amy E. Ubelhor. Thank you for adding your gifts of design, dimension and color to my vision.

Made in the USA
Monee, IL
15 September 2025